OECD/G20 Base Erosion and Profit Shifting Project

Making Dispute Resolution More Effective – MAP Peer Review Report, The Bahamas (Stage 2)

INCLUSIVE FRAMEWORK ON BEPS: ACTION 14

))OECD

BETTER POLICIES FOR BETTER LIVES

This document, as well as any data and map included herein, are without prejudice to the status of or sovereignty over any territory, to the delimitation of international frontiers and boundaries and to the name of any territory, city or area.

Please cite this publication as:
OECD (2022), *Making Dispute Resolution More Effective – MAP Peer Review Report, The Bahamas (Stage 2): Inclusive Framework on BEPS: Action 14*, OECD/G20 Base Erosion and Profit Shifting Project, OECD Publishing, Paris, https://doi.org/10.1787/3e3d34d5-en.

ISBN 978-92-64-85994-4 (print)
ISBN 978-92-64-95835-7 (pdf)

OECD/G20 Base Erosion and Profit Shifting Project
ISSN 2313-2604 (print)
ISSN 2313-2612 (online)

Foreword

Digitalisation and globalisation have had a profound impact on economies and the lives of people around the world, and this impact has only accelerated in the 21st century. These changes have brought with them challenges to the rules for taxing international business income, which have prevailed for more than a hundred years and created opportunities for base erosion and profit shifting (BEPS), requiring bold moves by policy makers to restore confidence in the system and ensure that profits are taxed where economic activities take place and value is created.

In 2013, the OECD ramped up efforts to address these challenges in response to growing public and political concerns about tax avoidance by large multinationals. The OECD and G20 countries joined forces and developed an Action Plan to address BEPS in September 2013. The Action Plan identified 15 actions aimed at introducing coherence in the domestic rules that affect cross-border activities, reinforcing substance requirements in the existing international standards, and improving transparency as well as certainty.

After two years of work, measures in response to the 15 actions, including those published in an interim form in 2014, were consolidated into a comprehensive package and delivered to G20 Leaders in November 2015. The BEPS package represents the first substantial renovation of the international tax rules in almost a century. As the BEPS measures are implemented, it is expected that profits will be reported where the economic activities that generate them are carried out and where value is created. BEPS planning strategies that rely on outdated rules or on poorly co-ordinated domestic measures will be rendered ineffective.

OECD and G20 countries also agreed to continue to work together to ensure a consistent and co-ordinated implementation of the BEPS recommendations and to make the project more inclusive. As a result, they created the OECD/G20 Inclusive Framework on BEPS (Inclusive Framework), bringing all interested and committed countries and jurisdictions on an equal footing in the Committee on Fiscal Affairs and its subsidiary bodies. With over 140 members, the Inclusive Framework monitors and peer reviews the implementation of the minimum standards and is completing the work on standard setting to address BEPS issues. In addition to its members, other international organisations and regional tax bodies are involved in the work of the Inclusive Framework, which also consults business and the civil society on its different work streams.

Although implementation of the BEPS package is dramatically changing the international tax landscape and improving the fairness of tax systems, one of the key outstanding BEPS issues – to address the tax challenges arising from the digitalisation of the economy – remained unresolved. In a major step forward on 8 October 2021, over 135 Inclusive Framework members, representing more than 95% of global GDP, joined a two-pillar solution to reform the international taxation rules and ensure that multinational enterprises pay a fair share of tax wherever they operate and generate profits in today's digitalised and globalised world economy. The implementation of these new rules is envisaged by 2023.

This report was approved by the Inclusive Framework on 17 March 2022 and prepared for publication by the OECD Secretariat.

Table of contents

Abbreviations and acronyms

APA	Advance Pricing Arrangement
FTA	Forum on Tax Administration
MAP	Mutual Agreement Procedure
OECD	Organisation for Economic Co-operation and Development

Executive summary

The Bahamas only has one tax treaty. The Bahamas has no experience with resolving MAP cases, as it has not been involved in any cases. The Bahamas reported that it has no direct tax system and does not impose income, corporate, capital or other direct taxes. This specific situation makes it unlikely, under its current tax system that the Bahamas takes an action that results in taxation not in accordance with any tax treaty it has entered into. However, the Bahamas reported that it is ready to resolve tax treaty-related disputes that would arise after an action being taken by its treaty partner.

Overall the Bahamas meets the majority of the elements of the Action 14 Minimum Standard. Where it has deficiencies, the Bahamas worked to address some of them, which has been monitored in stage 2 of the process. In this respect, the Bahamas solved some of the identified deficiencies.

The one tax treaty of the Bahamas contains a provision relating to MAP. The treaty follows paragraphs 1 through 3 of Article 25 of the OECD Model Tax Convention (OECD, 2017) and is consistent with the requirements of the Action 14 Minimum Standard. Therefore, there is no need for modifications in relation to tax treaty elements.

As the Bahamas has no bilateral APA programme in place, there were no further elements to assess regarding the prevention of disputes.

The Bahamas meets most of the requirements regarding availability and access to MAP under the Action 14 Minimum Standard. It provides access to MAP in all eligible cases, although it has since 1 January 2017 not received any MAP requests. Furthermore, the Bahamas has in place a documented bilateral notification process for those situations in which its competent authority considers the objection raised by taxpayers in a MAP request as not justified. However, the Bahamas has not yet issued MAP guidance, and its MAP profile contains only limited information.

Furthermore, the Bahamas has not been involved in any MAP cases during the period 2017-20, but it meets in principle all the requirements under the Action 14 Minimum Standard in relation to the resolution of MAP cases.

Lastly, the Bahamas in principle meets the Action 14 Minimum Standard as regards the implementation of MAP agreements. Since the Bahamas did not enter into any MAP agreements that required implementation by the Bahamas in 2017-20, no problems have surfaced regarding the implementation throughout the peer review process.

Reference

OECD (2017), *Model Tax Convention on Income and on Capital 2017 (Full Version)*, OECD Publishing, Paris, https://dx.doi.org/10.1787/g2g972ee-en.

Introduction

Available mechanisms in the Bahamas to resolve tax treaty-related disputes

The Bahamas has entered into one tax treaty on income (and/or capital), which is in force.[1] This treaty is being applied to one jurisdiction. It provides for a mutual agreement procedure for resolving disputes on the interpretation and application of the provisions of the tax treaty. The treaty is limited in scope.

The Bahamas reported that it has no direct tax system and does not impose income, corporate, capital or other direct taxes. This specific situation makes it unlikely, under its current tax system that the Bahamas takes an action that results in taxation not in accordance with any tax treaty it has entered into. The Bahamas further reported that it is however ready to resolve tax treaty-related disputes that would arise after an action being taken by its treaty partner. It noted that there are no domestic remedies available in the Bahamas.

In the Bahamas, the competent authority function to conduct the mutual agreement procedure ("**MAP**") is assigned to the Minister of Finance or an authorised representative of the Minister. This has been delegated to the Financial Secretary. The Bahamas reported that the Ministry of Finance, in particular the Office of the Financial Secretary and Department of Inland Revenue address issues related to matters falling within the ambit of taxation, in the first instance, pursuant to the relevant provision of the applicable treaty or domestic law in the absence of a treaty or convention.

The Bahamas has not yet issued guidance on the governance and administration of the mutual agreement procedure ("**MAP guidance**").

Developments in the Bahamas since 1 September 2019

Developments in relation to the tax treaty network

The stage 1 peer review report of the Bahamas noted that it was not conducting any tax treaty negotiations, and therefore there are no pending tax treaties to conclude. The Bahamas clarified that this situation remains the same. There is no need to modify the treaty the Bahamas has entered into.

Other developments

The Bahamas reported that the Legal and Regulatory Affairs Unit was established in the Ministry of Finance to assist with MAP matters.

Basis for the peer review process

Outline of the peer review process

The peer review process entails an evaluation of the Bahamas' implementation of the Action 14 Minimum Standard through an analysis of its legal and administrative framework relating to the mutual agreement procedure, as governed by its tax treaties, domestic legislation and regulations, as well as its MAP programme guidance (if any) and the practical application of that framework. The review process performed is desk-based and conducted through specific questionnaires completed by the Bahamas, its peers and taxpayers.

The process consists of two stages: a peer review process (stage 1) and a peer monitoring process (stage 2). In stage 1, the Bahamas' implementation of the Action 14 Minimum Standard as outlined above is evaluated, which has been reflected in a peer review report that has been adopted by the BEPS Inclusive Framework on 12 May 2020. This report identifies the strengths and shortcomings of the Bahamas in relation to the implementation of this standard and provides for recommendations on how these shortcomings should be addressed. The stage 1 report is published on the website of the OECD.[2] Stage 2 is launched within one year upon the adoption of the peer review report by the BEPS Inclusive Framework through an update report by the Bahamas. In this update report, the Bahamas reflected (i) what steps it has already taken, or are to be taken, to address any of the shortcomings identified in the peer review report and (ii) any plans or changes to its legislative and/or administrative framework concerning the implementation of the Action 14 Minimum Standard. The update report forms the basis for the completion of the peer review process, which is reflected in this update to the stage 1 peer review report.

Outline of the treaty analysis

For the purpose of this report and the statistics below, in assessing whether the Bahamas is compliant with the elements of the Action 14 Minimum Standard that relate to a specific treaty provision, the treaty as modified by a protocol was taken into account, even if it concerned a modification or a replacement of an existing treaty. Reference is made to Annex A for the overview of the Bahamas' tax treaty regarding the mutual agreement procedure.

Timing of the process and input received by peers and taxpayers

Stage 1 of the peer review process was for the Bahamas launched on 30 August 2019, with the sending of questionnaires to the Bahamas and its peers. The FTA MAP Forum has approved the stage 1 peer review report of the Bahamas in March 2020, with the subsequent approval by the BEPS Inclusive Framework on 12 May 2020. On 12 May 2021, the Bahamas submitted its update report, which initiated stage 2 of the process.

The period for evaluating the Bahamas' implementation of the Action 14 Minimum Standard ranges from 1 January 2017 to 31 August 2019 and formed the basis for the stage 1 peer review report. The period of review for stage 2 started on 1 September 2019 and depicts all developments as from that date until 30 April 2021.

No peers have provided input during both stage 1 and stage 2 on the Bahamas' implementation of the Action 14 Minimum Standard. This can be explained by the fact that the Bahamas' competent authority has never been involved in a MAP case as it has never received a MAP request from a taxpayer or from another competent authority.

Input by the Bahamas and co-operation throughout the process

During stage 1, the Bahamas provided extensive answers in its questionnaire. The Bahamas was responsive in the course of the drafting of the peer review report by responding to requests for additional information, and provided further clarity where necessary. In addition, the Bahamas provided the following information:

- MAP profile[3]
- MAP statistics[4] for 2018-20 (see below).

Concerning stage 2 of the process, the Bahamas submitted its update report on time and the information included therein was extensive. The Bahamas was co-operative during stage 2 and the finalisation of the peer review process.

Finally, the Bahamas is a member of the FTA MAP Forum and has shown good co-operation during the peer review process.

Overview of MAP caseload in the Bahamas

The analysis of the Bahamas' MAP caseload for stage 1 relates to the period starting on 1 January 2017 and ending on 31 December 2018. For stage 2 the period ranges from 1 January 2019 to 31 December 2020. Both periods are taken into account in this report for analysing the MAP statistics of the Bahamas. The analysis of the Bahamas' MAP caseload therefore relates to the period starting on 1 January 2017 and ending 31 December 2020 ("**Statistics Reporting Period**"). According to the statistics provided by the Bahamas, as mentioned above, the Bahamas has not been involved in any MAP cases during the Statistics Reporting Period.

General outline of the peer review report

This report includes an evaluation of the Bahamas' implementation of the Action 14 Minimum Standard. The report comprises the following four sections:

A. Preventing disputes

B. Availability and access to MAP

C. Resolution of MAP cases

D. Implementation of MAP agreements.

Each of these sections is divided into elements of the Action 14 Minimum Standard, as described in the terms of reference to monitor and review the implementing of the BEPS Action 14 Minimum Standard to make dispute resolution mechanisms more effective ("**Terms of Reference**").[5] Furthermore, the report depicts the changes adopted and plans shared by the Bahamas to implement elements of the Action 14 Minimum Standard where relevant. The conclusion of each element identifies areas for improvement (if any) and provides for recommendations how the specific area for improvement should be addressed.

The basis of this report is the outcome of the stage 1 peer review process, which has identified in each element areas for improvement (if any) and provides for recommendations how the specific area for improvement should be addressed. Following the outcome of the peer monitoring process of stage 2, each of the elements has been updated with a recent development section to reflect any actions taken or changes made on how recommendations have been addressed, or to reflect other changes in the legal and administrative framework of the Bahamas relating to the implementation of the Action 14 Minimum Standard. Where it concerns changes to MAP guidance or statistics, these changes are reflected in the analysis sections of the elements, with a general description of the changes in the recent development sections.

The objective of the Action 14 Minimum Standard is to make dispute resolution mechanisms more effective and concerns a continuous effort. Where recommendations have been fully implemented, this has been reflected and the conclusion section of the relevant element has been modified accordingly, but the Bahamas should continue to act in accordance with a given element of the Action 14 Minimum Standard, even if there is no area for improvement for this specific element.

Notes

1. The tax treaties the Bahamas has entered into are available at: https://www.bahamas.gov.bs/wps/portal/public/International%20Agreements/!ut/p/b1/vZLbkqIwFEW_pT_AJoEQwmMUsbkEEMLlxUKRFhTwjvL17VR11VyqxnmZ7pynVK1z9tk7ETIhEbl2v1bv-bnq2nz3457hhQRmjFJE2EwGGBihZ1NPeRNdKD-A9AGAvxwKnvZbohALCU_vN60zen0aLTZ5VJMb0lNYPBaY9naF-0Y31wESybSpSdmc2rl0vgwnUafzpZ2HYFCpeVUX3qBrW99E041M8hBznRdpU0pmVi2uuzyqcv3uZkWRoHrU7QrD5UeYVHlOR-tAcTbvR9zQYR_GjcljZ4s3kbHkS1P3TJN3qgcnxnlUREQu68vy0MTU__ILBaypwgCn8CTWJ23rlkL6QNTfpnDIwAMCKgfwDkgDhS4kAC0COr73hi2g18PPnN4ZLBhcgda2DtbJXbC7cDOExjYvgF5eGPa2OPcsYIj67lje0Xkh2NKR2yeqH8KuiJXH4ITiK1QBgFAXy04k13ySErhHpVFMHPhdwtK3xrpzHPB1zv87dOg-f9_Q1PIqmXz2q-aV_BKVAxlhSCVYIAQUYSoTrE6OZl0aviluRJj-ZiLE2RUIpbGLIWn7TlcSeNR4vhlKdVMdDo7KrXLwCznUPi7ab_p5syKQnzO43a5pqchuozp4KuIqpPVY8-Z1rZLymHQ9xXuxjUuz0Xp3WiSxFir-Xo9rmRcEDFIZPkq3f3cUg3ohCqpidZam1Gj-qhNGSUrYpXvXWYbo_jgKnPz7XQw95Qd7uAi7aLFfc-zehaUAmAdHoR9k14tbFPnPJnMfry8gGG0Mov/dl4/d5/L2dBISEvZ0FBIS9nQSEh/. Reference is made to Annex A for the overview of the Bahamas' tax treaties.

2. Available at: https://www.oecd.org/tax/beps/making-dispute-resolution-more-effective-map-peer-review-report-the-bahamas-stage-1-e6458e06-en.htm.

3. Available at https://www.oecd.org/tax/dispute/The-Bahamas-Dispute-Resolution-Profile.pdf.

4. The MAP statistics of the Bahamas are included in Annexes B and C of this report.

5. Terms of reference to monitor and review the implementing of the BEPS Action 14 Minimum Standard to make dispute resolution mechanisms more effective. Available at: www.oecd.org/tax/beps/beps-action-14-on-more-effective-dispute-resolution-peer-review-documents.pdf.

Part A

Preventing disputes

[A.1] **Include Article 25(3), first sentence, of the OECD Model Tax Convention in tax treaties**

> Jurisdictions should ensure that their tax treaties contain a provision which requires the competent authority of their jurisdiction to endeavour to resolve by mutual agreement any difficulties or doubts arising as to the interpretation or application of their tax treaties.

1.   Cases may arise concerning the interpretation or the application of tax treaties that do not necessarily relate to individual cases, but are more of a general nature. Inclusion of the first sentence of Article 25(3) of the OECD Model Tax Convention (OECD, 2017a) in tax treaties invites and authorises competent authorities to solve these cases, which may avoid submission of MAP requests and/or future disputes from arising, and which may reinforce the consistent bilateral application of tax treaties.

Current situation of the Bahamas' tax treaties

2.   The one tax treaty of the Bahamas contains a provision equivalent to Article 25(3), first sentence, of the OECD Model Tax Convention (OECD, 2017a) requiring their competent authority to endeavour to resolve by mutual agreement any difficulties or doubts arising as to the interpretation or application of the tax treaty.

3.   No peer input was provided during stage 1.

Recent developments

Bilateral modifications

4.   There are no recent developments as to new treaties or amendments to existing treaties being signed in relation to element A.1.

Peer input

5.   No peer input was provided.

Anticipated modifications

6.   The Bahamas reported it will seek to include Article 25(3), first sentence, of the OECD Model Tax Convention (OECD, 2017a) in all of its future tax treaties.

Conclusion

	Areas for improvement	Recommendations
[A.1]	-	-

[A.2] Provide roll-back of bilateral APAs in appropriate cases

> Jurisdictions with bilateral advance pricing arrangement ("APA") programmes should provide for the roll-back of APAs in appropriate cases, subject to the applicable time limits (such as statutes of limitation for assessment) where the relevant facts and circumstances in the earlier tax years are the same and subject to the verification of these facts and circumstances on audit.

7.   An APA is an arrangement that determines, in advance of controlled transactions, an appropriate set of criteria (e.g. method, comparables and appropriate adjustment thereto, critical assumptions as to future events) for the determination of the transfer pricing for those transactions over a fixed period of time.[1] The methodology to be applied prospectively under a bilateral or multilateral APA may be relevant in determining the treatment of comparable controlled transactions in previous filed years. The "roll-back" of an APA to these previous filed years may be helpful to prevent or resolve potential transfer pricing disputes.

The Bahamas' APA programme

8.   The Bahamas does not have an APA programme, by which there is no possibility for providing roll-back of bilateral APAs to previous years.

Recent developments

9.   There are no recent developments with respect to element A.2.

Practical application of roll-back of bilateral APAs

Period 1 January 2017-31 August 2019 (stage 1)

10.   The Bahamas reported in the period 1 January 2017-31 August 2019 it received no requests for bilateral APAs.

11.   No peer input was provided.

Period 1 September 2019-30 April 2021 (stage 2)

12.   The Bahamas reported that since 1 September 2019 it has also not received any bilateral APA requests.

13.   No peer input was provided.

Anticipated modifications

14.   The Bahamas did not indicate that it anticipates any modifications in relation to element A.2.

Conclusion

	Areas for improvement	Recommendations
[A.2]	-	-

Note

1. This description of an APA based on the definition of an APA in the OECD Transfer Pricing Guidelines for Multinational Enterprises and Tax Administrations (OECD, 2017b).

References

OECD (2017a), *Model Tax Convention on Income and on Capital 2017 (Full Version)*, OECD Publishing, Paris, https://dx.doi.org/10.1787/g2g972ee-en.

OECD (2017b), *OECD Transfer Pricing Guidelines for Multinational Enterprises and Tax Administrations 2017*, https://dx.doi.org/10.1787/tpg-2017-en.

Part B

Availability and access to MAP

[B.1]   Include Article 25(1) of the OECD Model Tax Convention in tax treaties

> Jurisdictions should ensure that their tax treaties contain a MAP provision which provides that when the taxpayer considers that the actions of one or both of the Contracting Parties result or will result for the taxpayer in taxation not in accordance with the provisions of the tax treaty, the taxpayer, may irrespective of the remedies provided by the domestic law of those Contracting Parties, make a request for MAP assistance, and that the taxpayer can present the request within a period of no less than three years from the first notification of the action resulting in taxation not in accordance with the provisions of the tax treaty.

15.   For resolving cases of taxation not in accordance with the provisions of the tax treaty, it is necessary that tax treaties include a provision allowing taxpayers to request a mutual agreement procedure and that this procedure can be requested irrespective of the remedies provided by the domestic law of the treaty partners. In addition, to provide certainty to taxpayers and competent authorities on the availability of the mutual agreement procedure, a minimum period of three years for submission of a MAP request, beginning on the date of the first notification of the action resulting in taxation not in accordance with the provisions of the tax treaty, is the baseline.

Current situation of Bahamas' tax treaties

Inclusion of Article 25(1), first sentence of the OECD Model Tax Convention

16.   The one tax treaty of the Bahamas does not contain a provision equivalent to Article 25(1), first sentence, of the OECD Model Tax Convention (OECD, 2017) as it read prior to or after the adoption of the Action 14 final report (OECD, 2015a), allowing taxpayers to submit a MAP request to the competent authority of the state in which they are resident or of either state when they consider that the actions of one or both of the treaty partners result or will result for the taxpayer in taxation not in accordance with the provisions of the tax treaty and that can be requested irrespective of the remedies provided by domestic law of either state.

17.   The tax treaty is considered not to have the full equivalent of Article 25(1), first sentence, of the OECD Model Tax Convention (OECD, 2015b) as it read prior to the adoption of the Action 14 final report (OECD, 2015a), since taxpayers are not allowed to submit a MAP request in the state of which they are a national where the case comes under the non-discrimination article. However, since the treaty does not contain a

non-discrimination provision and only applies to residents of one of the contracting states, it is considered to be in line with this part of element B.1.

Inclusion of Article 25(1), second sentence of the OECD Model Tax Convention

18.   The one tax treaty of the Bahamas contains a provision equivalent to Article 25(1), second sentence, of the OECD Model Tax Convention (OECD, 2017) allowing taxpayers to submit a MAP request within a period of no less than three years from the first notification of the action resulting in taxation not in accordance with the provisions of the particular tax treaty.

Peer input

19.   No peer input was provided during stage 1.

Practical application

Article 25(1), first sentence, of the OECD Model Tax Convention

20.   The Bahamas' tax treaty contains a provision allowing taxpayers to file a MAP request irrespective of domestic remedies. As the Bahamas reported that there are no direct taxes and no domestic remedies in the Bahamas, there would be no cases where a taxpayer would submit the issue at stake for a potential MAP case to the Bahamas' domestic remedies.

Recent developments

Bilateral modifications

21.   There are no recent developments as to new treaties or amendments to existing treaties being signed in relation to element B.1.

Peer input

22.   No peer input was provided.

Anticipated modifications

23.   The Bahamas reported it will seek to include Article 25(1) of the OECD Model Tax Convention (OECD, 2017), as amended by the Action 14 final report (OECD, 2015a), in all of its future tax treaties.

Conclusion

	Areas for improvement	Recommendations
[B.1]	-	-

[B.2] Allow submission of MAP requests to the competent authority of either treaty partner, or, alternatively, introduce a bilateral consultation or notification process

> Jurisdictions should ensure that either (i) their tax treaties contain a provision which provides that the taxpayer can make a request for MAP assistance to the competent authority of either Contracting Party, or (ii) where the treaty does not permit a MAP request to be made to either Contracting Party and the competent authority who received the MAP request from the taxpayer does not consider the taxpayer's objection to be justified, the competent authority should implement a bilateral consultation or notification process which allows the other competent authority to provide its views on the case (such consultation shall not be interpreted as consultation as to how to resolve the case).

24.   In order to ensure that all competent authorities concerned are aware of MAP requests submitted, for a proper consideration of the request by them and to ensure that taxpayers have effective access to MAP in eligible cases, it is essential that all tax treaties contain a provision that either allows taxpayers to submit a MAP request to the competent authority:

i.   of either treaty partner; or, in the absence of such provision,

ii.   where it is a resident, or to the competent authority of the state of which they are a national if their cases come under the non-discrimination article. In such cases, jurisdictions should have in place a bilateral consultation or notification process where a competent authority considers the objection raised by the taxpayer in a MAP request as being not justified.

Domestic bilateral consultation or notification process in place

25.   As discussed under element B.1, the one tax treaty of the Bahamas currently does not contain a provision equivalent to Article 25(1), first sentence, of the OECD Model Tax Convention (OECD, 2017) as changed by the Action 14 final report (OECD, 2015a), allowing taxpayers to submit a MAP request to the competent authority of either treaty partner.

26.   The Bahamas reported that it has introduced a bilateral consultation or notification process that allows the other competent authority concerned to provide its views on the case when the Bahamas' competent authority considers the objection raised in the MAP request not to be justified.

Recent developments

27.   The Bahamas reported that it has introduced a documented bilateral consultation or notification process for those situations where its competent authority would consider the objection raised in a MAP request as not being justified.

Practical application

Period 1 January 2017-31 August 2019 (stage 1)

28.   The Bahamas reported that in the period 1 January 2017-31 August 2019 its competent authority has not received any MAP requests. Therefore, there were no cases where it was decided that the objection raised by taxpayers in such request was not justified.

29.   No peer input was provided.

Period 1 September 2019-30 April 2021 (stage 2)

30.   The Bahamas reported that since 1 September 2019 it has also not received any MAP requests. Therefore, there were no cases where it was decided that the objection raised by taxpayers in such request was not justified.

31.   No peer input was provided.

Anticipated modifications

32.   The Bahamas did not indicate that it anticipates any modifications in relation to element B.2.

Conclusion

	Areas for improvement	Recommendations
[B.2]	-	-

[B.3] Provide access to MAP in transfer pricing cases

Jurisdictions should provide access to MAP in transfer pricing cases.

33.   Where two or more tax administrations take different positions on what constitutes arm's length conditions for specific transactions between associated enterprises, economic double taxation may occur. Not granting access to MAP with respect to a treaty partner's transfer pricing adjustment, with a view to eliminating the economic double taxation that may arise from such adjustment, will likely frustrate the main objective of tax treaties. Jurisdictions should thus provide access to MAP in transfer pricing cases.

Legal and administrative framework

34.   The one tax treaty of the Bahamas does not contain a provision on associated enterprises, based on Article 9 of the OECD Model Tax Convention (OECD, 2017). Therefore, transfer pricing cases would not be covered by the treaty.

Recent developments

Bilateral modifications

35.   There are no recent developments as to new treaties or amendments to existing treaties being signed in relation to element B.3.

Application of legal and administrative framework in practice

Period 1 January 2017-31 August 2019 (stage 1)

36.   The Bahamas reported that in the period 1 January 2017-31 August 2019 it has received no MAP requests for transfer pricing cases.

37.   No peer input was provided.

Period 1 September 2019-30 April 2021 (stage 2)

38.   The Bahamas reported that it has also received no MAP requests for transfer pricing cases since 1 September 2019.

39.   No peer input was provided.

Anticipated modifications

40.   The Bahamas did not indicate that it anticipates any modifications in relation to element B.3.

Conclusion

	Areas for improvement	Recommendations
[B.3]	-	-

[B.4]   Provide access to MAP in relation to the application of anti-abuse provisions

> Jurisdictions should provide access to MAP in cases in which there is a disagreement between the taxpayer and the tax authorities making the adjustment as to whether the conditions for the application of a treaty anti-abuse provision have been met or as to whether the application of a domestic law anti-abuse provision is in conflict with the provisions of a treaty.

41.   There is no general rule denying access to MAP in cases of perceived abuse. In order to protect taxpayers from arbitrary application of anti-abuse provisions in tax treaties and in order to ensure that competent authorities have a common understanding on such application, it is important that taxpayers have access to MAP if they consider the interpretation and/or application of a treaty anti-abuse provision as being incorrect. Subsequently, to avoid cases in which the application of domestic anti-abuse legislation is in conflict with the provisions of a tax treaty, it is also important that taxpayers have access to MAP in such cases.

Legal and administrative framework

42.   The one tax treaty of the Bahamas does not contain an anti-abuse provision and no domestic anti-abuse provision would apply as there are no income taxes in the Bahamas.

43.   In that regard, no cases in which there is a disagreement between the taxpayer and the tax authorities making the adjustment as to whether the conditions for the application of a treaty anti-abuse provision have been met or as to whether the application of a domestic law anti-abuse provision is in conflict with the provisions of a treaty can occur based on actions taken by the Bahamas.

Recent developments

44.   There are no recent developments with respect to element B.4.

Practical application

Period 1 January 2017-31 August 2019 (stage 1)

45. The Bahamas reported that in the period 1 January 2017-31 August 2019 it has not received any MAP requests from taxpayers.

46. No peer input was provided.

Period 1 September 2019-30 April 2021 (stage 2)

47. The Bahamas reported that since 1 September 2019 it has also not received any MAP requests from taxpayers.

48. No peer input was provided.

Anticipated modifications

49. The Bahamas did not indicate that it anticipates any modifications in relation to element B.4.

Conclusion

	Areas for improvement	Recommendations
[B.4]	-	-

[B.5] Provide access to MAP in cases of audit settlements

> Jurisdictions should not deny access to MAP in cases where there is an audit settlement between tax authorities and taxpayers. If jurisdictions have an administrative or statutory dispute settlement/resolution process independent from the audit and examination functions and that can only be accessed through a request by the taxpayer, jurisdictions may limit access to the MAP with respect to the matters resolved through that process.

50. An audit settlement procedure can be valuable to taxpayers by providing certainty on their tax position. Nevertheless, as double taxation may not be fully eliminated by agreeing on such settlements, taxpayers should have access to the MAP in such cases, unless they were already resolved via an administrative or statutory disputes settlement/resolution process that functions independently from the audit and examination function and which is only accessible through a request by taxpayers.

Legal and administrative framework

Audit settlements

51. The Bahamas has no direct taxes and therefore audit settlements are not applicable.

Administrative or statutory dispute settlement/resolution process

52.   The Bahamas reported it does not have an administrative or statutory dispute settlement/resolution process in place, which is independent from the audit and examination functions and which can only be accessed through a request by the taxpayer.

Recent developments

53.   There are no recent developments with respect to element B.5.

Practical application

Period 1 January 2017-31 August 2019 (stage 1)

54.   The Bahamas reported that in the period 1 January 2017-31 August 2019 it has not received any MAP requests from taxpayers.

55.   No peer input was provided.

Period 1 September 2019-30 April 2021 (stage 2)

56.   The Bahamas reported that since 1 September 2019 it has also not received any MAP requests from taxpayers.

57.   No peer input was provided.

Anticipated modifications

58.   The Bahamas did not indicate that it anticipates any modifications in relation to element B.5.

Conclusion

	Areas for improvement	Recommendations
[B.5]	-	-

[B.6]   Provide access to MAP if required information is submitted

> Jurisdictions should not limit access to MAP based on the argument that insufficient information was provided if the taxpayer has provided the required information based on the rules, guidelines and procedures made available to taxpayers on access to and the use of MAP.

59.   To resolve cases where there is taxation not in accordance with the provisions of the tax treaty, it is important that competent authorities do not limit access to MAP when taxpayers have complied with the information and documentation requirements as provided in the jurisdiction's guidance relating hereto. Access to MAP will be facilitated when such required information and documentation is made publicly available.

Legal framework on access to MAP and information to be submitted

60.   As will be discussed under element B.8, the Bahamas has not yet issued any MAP guidance.

61.   The Bahamas reported that it will provide access to MAP in all cases where taxpayers have complied with the information or documentation its competent authority asks the taxpayer to provide, although it does not have any rules or timelines in place regarding requesting additional information to process a MAP request where a taxpayer has not included all required information in its MAP request.

Recent developments

62.   There are no recent developments with respect to element B.6.

Practical application

Period 1 January 2017-31 August 2019 (stage 1)

63.   The Bahamas reported that in the period 1 January 2017-31 August 2019 it has not received any MAP requests from a taxpayer and therefore has not denied access to MAP for cases where the taxpayer had provided the information or documentation its competent authority asks the taxpayer to provide.

64.   No peer input was provided.

Period 1 September 2019-30 April 2021 (stage 2)

65.   The Bahamas reported that since 1 September 2019 it has not received any MAP requests and therefore has also not denied access to MAP for cases where the taxpayer had provided the information or documentation its competent authority asks the taxpayer to provide.

66.   No peer input was provided.

Anticipated modifications

67.   The Bahamas did not indicate that it anticipates any modifications in relation to element B.6.

Conclusion

	Areas for improvement	Recommendations
[B.6]	-	-

[B.7]   Include Article 25(3), second sentence, of the OECD Model Tax Convention in tax treaties

> Jurisdictions should ensure that their tax treaties contain a provision under which competent authorities may consult together for the elimination of double taxation in cases not provided for in their tax treaties.

68.   For ensuring that tax treaties operate effectively and in order for competent authorities to be able to respond quickly to unanticipated situations, it is useful that tax treaties include the second sentence of Article 25(3) of the OECD Model Tax Convention (OECD, 2017), enabling them to consult together for the elimination of double taxation in cases not provided for by these treaties.

Current situation of Bahamas' tax treaties

69.   The one tax treaty of the Bahamas does not contain a provision equivalent to Article 25(3), second sentence, of the OECD Model Tax Convention (OECD, 2017) allowing their competent authorities to consult together for the elimination of double taxation in cases not provided for in their tax treaty.

70.   The treaty, however, has a limited scope of application. This concerns a tax treaty that only applies to a certain category of income or a certain category of taxpayers, whereby the structure and articles of the OECD Model Tax Convention (OECD, 2017) are not followed. As the treaty was intentionally negotiated with a limited scope, the inclusion of Article 25(3), second sentence, of the OECD Model Tax Convention (OECD, 2017) would contradict the object and purpose of the treaty and such inclusion would also be inappropriate, as it would allow competent authorities the possibility to consult in cases that have intentionally been excluded from the scope of a tax treaty. For this reason, therefore, there is a justification not to contain Article 25(3), second sentence, of the OECD Model Tax Convention (OECD, 2017) for the treaty with a limited scope of application.

71.   No peer input was provided during stage 1.

Recent developments

Bilateral modifications

72.   There are no recent developments as to new treaties or amendments to existing treaties being signed in relation to element B.7.

Peer input

73.   No peer input was provided.

Anticipated modifications

74.   The Bahamas reported it will seek to include Article 25(3), second sentence, of the OECD Model Tax Convention (OECD, 2017) in all of its future tax treaties, unless the treaties concerned are limited in scope, such that there is justification for them not to contain Article 25(3), second sentence, of the OECD Model Tax Convention (OECD, 2017).

Conclusion

	Areas for improvement	Recommendations
[B.7]	-	-

[B.8]   Publish clear and comprehensive MAP guidance

> Jurisdictions should publish clear rules, guidelines and procedures on access to and use of the MAP and include the specific information and documentation that should be submitted in a taxpayer's request for MAP assistance.

75.   Information on a jurisdiction's MAP regime facilitates the timely initiation and resolution of MAP cases. Clear rules, guidelines and procedures on access to and use of the MAP are essential for making taxpayers and other stakeholders aware of how a jurisdiction's MAP regime functions. In addition, to ensure that a MAP request is received and will be reviewed by the competent authority in a timely manner, it is important that a jurisdiction's MAP guidance clearly and comprehensively explains how a taxpayer can make a MAP request and what information and documentation should be included in such request.

The Bahamas' MAP guidance

76.   Since the Bahamas has not yet published MAP guidance, the information that the FTA MAP Forum agreed should be included in such guidance is not available. This concerns: (i) contact information of the competent authority or the office in charge of MAP cases and (ii) the manner and form in which the taxpayers should submit its MAP request.[1]

Information and documentation to be included in a MAP request

77.   To facilitate the review of a MAP request by competent authorities and to have more consistency in the required content of MAP requests, the FTA MAP Forum agreed on guidance that jurisdictions could use in their domestic guidance on what information and documentation taxpayers need to include in a request for MAP assistance.[2] This concerns:

- identity of the taxpayer(s) covered in the MAP request
- the basis for the request
- facts of the case
- analysis of the issue(s) requested to be resolved via MAP
- whether the MAP request was also submitted to the competent authority of the other treaty partner
- whether the MAP request was also submitted to another authority under another instrument that provides for a mechanism to resolve treaty-related disputes
- whether the issue(s) involved were dealt with previously
- a statement confirming that all information and documentation provided in the MAP request is accurate and that the taxpayer will assist the competent authority in its resolution of the issue(s) presented in the MAP request by furnishing any other information or documentation required by the competent authority in a timely manner.

78.   Due to the fact that the Bahamas has not issued MAP guidance, there is also no guidance on any of the above in the Bahamas, and as discussed under element B.6 no rules or timelines are in place for requesting additional information for a consideration of a MAP request by the competent authority and for taxpayers to provide such information.

Recent developments

79.   There are no recent developments with respect to element B.8.

Anticipated modifications

80.   The Bahamas indicated that it is currently in the process of drafting its MAP guidance.

Conclusion

	Areas for improvement	Recommendations
[B.8]	There is no published MAP guidance.	The Bahamas should, without further delay, introduce and publish guidance on access to and use of the MAP, and in particular include the contact information of its competent authority as well as the manner and form in which the taxpayer should submit its MAP request, including the documentation and information that should be included in such a request.

[B.9] Make MAP guidance available and easily accessible and publish MAP profile

> Jurisdictions should take appropriate measures to make rules, guidelines and procedures on access to and use of the MAP available and easily accessible to the public and should publish their jurisdiction MAP profiles on a shared public platform pursuant to the agreed template.

81.   The public availability and accessibility of a jurisdiction's MAP guidance increases public awareness on access to and the use of the MAP in that jurisdiction. Publishing MAP profiles on a shared public platform further promotes the transparency and dissemination of the MAP programme.[3]

Rules, guidelines and procedures on access to and use of the MAP

82.   As discussed under element B.8, the Bahamas has not yet published MAP guidance.

MAP profile

83.   The MAP profile of the Bahamas is published on the website of the OECD and was last updated in July 2021.[4] This MAP profile contains only minimal information and also does not include external links that could provide extra information and guidance where appropriate.

Recent developments

84.   The Bahamas has updated the contact details and treaties list on its MAP profile in July 2021.

Anticipated modifications

85.   The Bahamas did not indicate that it anticipates any modifications in relation to element B.9.

Conclusion

	Areas for improvement	Recommendations
[B.9]	There is no MAP guidance publicly available. Furthermore, the MAP profile of the Bahamas contains only limited information.	The Bahamas should make its MAP guidance publicly available and easily accessible once it has been introduced. Furthermore, the Bahamas should provide further details in its MAP profile.

[B.10] Clarify in MAP guidance that audit settlements do not preclude access to MAP

> Jurisdictions should clarify in their MAP guidance that audit settlements between tax authorities and taxpayers do not preclude access to MAP. If jurisdictions have an administrative or statutory dispute settlement/resolution process independent from the audit and examination functions and that can only be accessed through a request by the taxpayer, and jurisdictions limit access to the MAP with respect to the matters resolved through that process, jurisdictions should notify their treaty partners of such administrative or statutory processes and should expressly address the effects of those processes with respect to the MAP in their public guidance on such processes and in their public MAP programme guidance.

86.   As explained under element B.5, an audit settlement can be valuable to taxpayers by providing certainty to them on their tax position. Nevertheless, as double taxation may not be fully eliminated by agreeing with such settlements, it is important that a jurisdiction's MAP guidance clarifies that in case of audit settlement taxpayers have access to the MAP. In addition, for providing clarity on the relationship between administrative or statutory dispute settlement or resolution processes and the MAP (if any), it is critical that both the public guidance on such processes and the public MAP programme guidance address the effects of those processes, if any. Finally, as the MAP represents a collaborative approach between treaty partners, it is helpful that treaty partners are notified of each other's MAP programme and limitations thereto, particularly in relation to the previously mentioned processes.

MAP and audit settlements in the MAP guidance

87.   As previously discussed under B.5, audit settlements are not possible in the Bahamas. In that regard, there is no need to address in its MAP guidance that such settlements do not preclude access to MAP.

88.   No peer input was provided.

MAP and other administrative or statutory dispute settlement/resolution processes in available guidance

89.   As previously mentioned under element B.5, the Bahamas does not have an administrative or statutory dispute settlement/resolution process in place that is independent from the audit and examination functions and that can only be accessed through a request by the taxpayer. In that regard, there is no need to address the effects of such process with respect to MAP in the Bahamas' MAP guidance.

90.   No peer input was provided.

Notification of treaty partners of existing administrative or statutory dispute settlement/resolution processes

91.   As the Bahamas does not have an internal administrative or statutory dispute settlement/resolution process in place, there is no need for notifying treaty partners of such process.

Recent developments

92.   There are no recent developments with respect to element B.10.

Anticipated modifications

93.   The Bahamas did not indicate that it anticipates any modifications in relation to element B.10.

Conclusion

	Areas for improvement	Recommendations
[B.10]	-	-

Notes

1.   Available at: www.oecd.org/tax/beps/beps-action-14-on-more-effective-dispute-resolution-peer-review-documents.pdf.

2.   Available at: www.oecd.org/tax/beps/beps-action-14-on-more-effective-dispute-resolution-peer-review-documents.pdf.

3.   The shared public platform can be found at: www.oecd.org/ctp/dispute/country-map-profiles.htm.

4.   Available at: https://www.oecd.org/tax/dispute/The-Bahamas-Dispute-Resolution-Profile.pdf.

References

OECD (2015a), *Model Tax Convention on Income and on Capital 2014 (Full Version)*, OECD Publishing, Paris, https://dx.doi.org/10.1787/9789264239081-en.

OECD (2015b), "Making Dispute Resolution Mechanisms More Effective, Action 14 – 2015 Final Report", in *OECD/G20 Base Erosion and Profit Shifting Project*, OECD Publishing, Paris, https://dx.doi.org/10.1787/9789264241633-en.

OECD (2017), *Model Tax Convention on Income and on Capital 2017 (Full Version)*, OECD Publishing, Paris, https://dx.doi.org/10.1787/g2g972ee-en.

Part C

Resolution of MAP cases

[C.1] **Include Article 25(2), first sentence, of the OECD Model Tax Convention in tax treaties**

> Jurisdictions should ensure that their tax treaties contain a provision which requires that the competent authority who receives a MAP request from the taxpayer, shall endeavour, if the objection from the taxpayer appears to be justified and the competent authority is not itself able to arrive at a satisfactory solution, to resolve the MAP case by mutual agreement with the competent authority of the other Contracting Party, with a view to the avoidance of taxation which is not in accordance with the tax treaty.

94.   It is of critical importance that in addition to allowing taxpayers to request for a MAP, tax treaties also include the equivalent of the first sentence of Article 25(2) of the OECD Model Tax Convention (OECD, 2017), which obliges competent authorities, in situations where the objection raised by taxpayers are considered justified and where cases cannot be unilaterally resolved, to enter into discussions with each other to resolve cases of taxation not in accordance with the provisions of a tax treaty.

Current situation of Bahamas' tax treaties

95.   The one tax treaty of the Bahamas contains a provision equivalent to Article 25(2), first sentence, of the OECD Model Tax Convention (OECD, 2017) requiring its competent authority to endeavour – when the objection raised is considered justified and no unilateral solution is possible – to resolve by mutual agreement with the competent authority of the other treaty partner the MAP case with a view to the avoidance of taxation which is not in accordance with the tax treaty.

96.   No peer input was provided during stage 1.

Recent developments

Bilateral modifications

97.   There are no recent developments as to new treaties or amendments to existing treaties being signed in relation to element C.1.

Peer input

98.   No peer input was provided.

Anticipated modifications

99. The Bahamas reported it will seek to include Article 25(2), first sentence, of the OECD Model Tax Convention (OECD, 2017) in all of its future tax treaties.

Conclusion

	Areas for improvement	Recommendations
[C.1]	-	-

[C.2] Seek to resolve MAP cases within a 24-month average timeframe

> Jurisdictions should seek to resolve MAP cases within an average time frame of 24 months. This time frame applies to both jurisdictions (i.e. the jurisdiction which receives the MAP request from the taxpayer and its treaty partner).

100. As double taxation creates uncertainties and leads to costs for both taxpayers and jurisdictions, and as the resolution of MAP cases may also avoid (potential) similar issues for future years concerning the same taxpayers, it is important that MAP cases are resolved swiftly. A period of 24 months is considered as an appropriate time period to resolve MAP cases on average.

Reporting of MAP statistics

101. The FTA MAP Forum has agreed on rules for reporting of MAP statistics ("**MAP Statistics Reporting Framework**") for MAP requests submitted on or after 1 January 2016 ("**post-2015 cases**"). Also, for MAP requests submitted prior to that date ("**pre-2016 cases**"), the FTA MAP Forum agreed to report MAP statistics on the basis of an agreed template. The Bahamas joined in the Inclusive Framework in 2017. For this reason the statistics referred to are pre-2017 cases for cases that were pending on 31 December 2016, and post-2016 cases for cases that started on or after 1 January 2017. The Bahamas provided its MAP statistics for 2018 in the course of this peer review and its MAP statistics for 2019-20 pursuant to the MAP Statistics Reporting Framework within the given deadline. The statistics discussed below include both pre-2017 and post-2016 cases and they are attached to this report as Annex B and Annex C respectively, showing that the Bahamas has not been involved in any MAP cases since 1 January 2017.

Monitoring of MAP statistics

102. The Bahamas does not have a system in place with its treaty partners that communicates, monitors and manages the MAP caseload, which can be explained by the fact that the Bahamas was never involved in a MAP case.

Analysis of the Bahamas' MAP caseload

103. The analysis of the Bahamas' MAP caseload relates to the period starting on 1 January 2017 and ending on 31 December 2020.

104. The Bahamas has not been involved in any MAP case during the Statistics Reporting Period.

Overview of cases closed during the Statistics Reporting Period

105.   The Bahamas has not been involved in any MAP case during the Statistics Reporting Period.

Average timeframe needed to resolve MAP cases

106.   The Bahamas has not been involved in any MAP case during the Statistics Reporting Period.

Peer input

107.   No peer input was provided during stage 1.

Recent developments

108.   The Bahamas was in the stage 1 peer review report under element C.2 recommended to report its MAP statistics annually. In this respect, the Bahamas submitted its 2019 and 2020 MAP statistics on time.

109.   No peer input was provided during stage 2.

Anticipated modifications

110.   The Bahamas did not indicate that it anticipates any modifications in relation to element C.2.

Conclusion

	Areas for improvement	Recommendations
[C.2]	-	-

[C.3] Provide adequate resources to the MAP function

> Jurisdictions should ensure that adequate resources are provided to the MAP function.

111.   Adequate resources, including personnel, funding and training, are necessary to properly perform the competent authority function and to ensure that MAP cases are resolved in a timely, efficient and effective manner.

Description of the Bahamas' competent authority

112.   Under the one tax treaty of the Bahamas, the competent authority function is assigned to the Minister of Finance or an authorised representative of the Minister. This has been delegated to the Financial Secretary. The Bahamas reported that the Ministry of Finance, in particular the Office of the Financial Secretary and Department of Inland Revenue addresses issues related to matters falling within the ambit of taxation, in the first instance, pursuant to the relevant provision of the applicable treaty or domestic law in the absence of a treaty or convention. Further, the Legal and Regulatory Affairs Unit in the Ministry of Finance will assist with MAP matters.

Monitoring mechanism

113. As discussed under element C.2, the Bahamas' competent authority has not yet been involved in any MAP cases, by which there were no MAP statistics available to analyse the pursued 24-month average.

Recent developments

114. The Bahamas reported that the Legal and Regulatory Affairs Unit was established in the Ministry of Finance to assist with MAP matters.

Practical application

MAP statistics

115. As discussed under element C.2, the Bahamas has not yet received any MAP requests, by which there were no MAP statistics available to analyse the pursued 24-month average.

Peer input

116. No peer input was provided during stage 1 (1 January 2017-31 August 2019) and stage 2 (1 September 2019-30 April 2021).

Anticipated modifications

117. The Bahamas did not indicate that it anticipates any modifications in relation to element C.3.

Conclusion

	Areas for improvement	Recommendations
[C.3]	-	-

[C.4] Ensure staff in charge of MAP has the authority to resolve cases in accordance with the applicable tax treaty

> Jurisdictions should ensure that the staff in charge of MAP processes have the authority to resolve MAP cases in accordance with the terms of the applicable tax treaty, in particular without being dependent on the approval or the direction of the tax administration personnel who made the adjustments at issue or being influenced by considerations of the policy that the jurisdictions would like to see reflected in future amendments to the treaty.

118. Ensuring that staff in charge of MAP can and will resolve cases, absent any approval/ direction by the tax administration personnel directly involved in the adjustment and absent any policy considerations, contributes to a principled and consistent approach to MAP cases.

Functioning of staff in charge of MAP

119. As discussed under element C.3, the Bahamas reported that MAP cases would be handled by the Office of the Financial Secretary and Department of Inland Revenue. The Bahamas clarified that its competent authority will take into consideration the actual

terms of a tax treaty as applicable for the relevant year and that it is committed not to be influenced by policy considerations that the Bahamas would like to see reflected in future amendments to the treaty.

120.   In regard of the above, the Bahamas reported that the staff in charge of MAP in the Bahamas would have the necessary authority to resolve MAP cases as it is not dependent on the approval/direction of outside personnel and there are no impediments in the Bahamas' abilities to perform its MAP functions.

Recent developments

121.   There are no recent developments with respect to element C.4.

Practical application

122.   No peer input was provided during stage 1 (1 January 2017-31 August 2019) and stage 2 (1 September 2019-30 April 2021).

Anticipated modifications

123.   The Bahamas did not indicate that it anticipates any modifications in relation to element C.4.

Conclusion

	Areas for improvement	Recommendations
[C.4]	-	-

[C.5] Use appropriate performance indicators for the MAP function

> Jurisdictions should not use performance indicators for their competent authority functions and staff in charge of MAP processes based on the amount of sustained audit adjustments or maintaining tax revenue.

124.   For ensuring that each case is considered on its individual merits and will be resolved in a principled and consistent manner, it is essential that any performance indicators for the competent authority function and for the staff in charge of MAP processes are appropriate and not based on the amount of sustained audit adjustments or aim at maintaining a certain amount of tax revenue.

Performance indicators used by the Bahamas

125.   The Action 14 final report (OECD, 2015) includes examples of performance indicators that are considered appropriate. These indicators are:

- number of MAP cases resolved

- consistency (i.e. a treaty should be applied in a principled and consistent manner to MAP cases involving the same facts and similarly-situated taxpayers)

- time taken to resolve a MAP case (recognising that the time taken to resolve a MAP case may vary according to its complexity and that matters not under the control of a competent authority may have a significant impact on the time needed to resolve a case).

126.   In view of these examples, as the Bahamas has not been involved in any MAP cases thus far, it did not report using any of these performance indicators to assess staff in charge of MAP cases.

127.   Further to the above, the Bahamas reported that it uses the Bahamas Public Service Assessment Criteria/Evaluations as staff performance indicators, and does not use any performance indicators for staff in charge of MAP that are related to the outcome of MAP discussions in terms of the amount of sustained audit adjustments or maintained tax revenue. In other words, staff in charge of MAP is not evaluated on the basis of the material outcome of MAP discussions.

Recent developments

128.   There are no recent developments with respect to element C.5.

Practical application

129.   No Peer input was provided during stage 1 (1 January 2017-31 August 2019) and stage 2 (1 September 2019-30 April 2021).

Anticipated modifications

130.   The Bahamas did not indicate that it anticipates any modifications in relation to element C.5.

Conclusion

	Areas for improvement	Recommendations
[C.5]	-	-

[C.6] Provide transparency with respect to the position on MAP arbitration

Jurisdictions should provide transparency with respect to their positions on MAP arbitration.

131.   The inclusion of an arbitration provision in tax treaties may help ensure that MAP cases are resolved within a certain timeframe, which provides certainty to both taxpayers and competent authorities. In order to have full clarity on whether arbitration as a final stage in the MAP process can and will be available in jurisdictions it is important that jurisdictions are transparent on their position on MAP arbitration.

Position on MAP arbitration

132.   The Bahamas reported that it has no position on MAP arbitration but it has no domestic law limitations for including MAP arbitration in its tax treaties.

Recent developments

133.   There are no recent developments with respect to element C.6.

Practical application

134.   The Bahamas has not incorporated an arbitration clause in its treaty as a final stage to the MAP.

Anticipated modifications

135.   The Bahamas did not indicate that it anticipates any modifications in relation to element C.6.

Conclusion

	Areas for improvement	Recommendations
[C.6]	-	-

References

OECD (2015), "Making Dispute Resolution Mechanisms More Effective, Action 14 – 2015 Final Report", in *OECD/G20 Base Erosion and Profit Shifting Project*, OECD Publishing, Paris, https://dx.doi.org/10.1787/9789264241633-en.

OECD (2017), *Model Tax Convention on Income and on Capital 2017 (Full Version)*, OECD Publishing, Paris, https://dx.doi.org/10.1787/g2g972ee-en.

Part D

Implementation of MAP agreements

[D.1] Implement all MAP agreements

> Jurisdictions should implement any agreement reached in MAP discussions, including by making appropriate adjustments to the tax assessed in transfer pricing cases.

136.   In order to provide full certainty to taxpayers and the jurisdictions, it is essential that all MAP agreements are implemented by the competent authorities concerned.

Legal framework to implement MAP agreements

137.   The Bahamas reported that it is unlikely that it would need to implement a MAP agreement as it has no direct tax system and does not impose income, corporate, capital or other direct taxes in the Bahamas.

Recent developments

138.   There are no recent developments with respect to element D.1.

Practical application

Period 1 January 2017-31 August 2019 (stage 1)

139.   As the Bahamas was not involved in any MAP cases in the period 1 January 2017-31 August 2019, it was not possible to assess the implementation of MAP agreements by the Bahamas.

140.   No peer input was provided.

Period 1 September 2019-30 April 2021 (stage 2)

141.   The Bahamas was also not involved in any MAP cases since 1 September 2019.

142.   No peer input was provided.

Anticipated modifications

143.   The Bahamas did not indicate that it anticipates any modifications in relation to element D.1.

Conclusion

	Areas for improvement	Recommendations
[D.1]	-	-

[D.2] Implement all MAP agreements on a timely basis

> Agreements reached by competent authorities through the MAP process should be implemented on a timely basis.

144. Delay of implementation of MAP agreements may lead to adverse financial consequences for both taxpayers and competent authorities. To avoid this and to increase certainty for all parties involved, it is important that the implementation of any MAP agreement is not obstructed by procedural and/or statutory delays in the jurisdictions concerned.

Theoretical timeframe for implementing mutual agreements

145. As discussed under element D.1, the Bahamas reported that it is unlikely that it would need to implement a MAP agreement as it has no direct taxes in the Bahamas.

Recent developments

146. There are no recent developments with respect to element D.2.

Practical application

Period 1 January 2017-31 August 2019 (stage 1)

147. As the Bahamas was not involved in any MAP cases in the period 1 January 2017-31 August 2019, it was not possible to assess the timely implementation of MAP agreements by the Bahamas.

148. No peer input was provided.

Period 1 September 2019-30 April 2021 (stage 2)

149. The Bahamas was also not involved in any MAP cases since 1 September 2019.

150. No peer input was provided.

Anticipated modifications

151. The Bahamas did not indicate that it anticipates any modifications in relation to element D.2.

Conclusion

	Areas for improvement	Recommendations
[D.2]	-	-

[D.3] Include Article 25(2), second sentence, of the OECD Model Tax Convention in tax treaties or alternative provisions in Article 9(1) and Article 7(2)

> Jurisdictions should either (i) provide in their tax treaties that any mutual agreement reached through MAP shall be implemented notwithstanding any time limits in their domestic law, or (ii) be willing to accept alternative treaty provisions that limit the time during which a Contracting Party may make an adjustment pursuant to Article 9(1) or Article 7(2), in order to avoid late adjustments with respect to which MAP relief will not be available.

152.   In order to provide full certainty to taxpayers it is essential that implementation of MAP agreements is not obstructed by any time limits in the domestic law of the jurisdictions concerned. Such certainty can be provided by either including the equivalent of Article 25(2), second sentence, of the OECD Model Tax Convention (OECD, 2017) in tax treaties, or alternatively, setting a time limit in Article 9(1) and Article 7(2) for making adjustments to avoid that late adjustments obstruct granting of MAP relief.

Legal framework and current situation of Bahamas' tax treaties

153.   As discussed under element D.1, the Bahamas reported that it is unlikely that it would need to implement a MAP agreement as it has no direct taxes in the Bahamas.

154.   The one tax treaty of the Bahamas contains a provision equivalent to Article 25(2), second sentence, of the OECD Model Tax Convention (OECD, 2017) that any mutual agreement reached through MAP shall be implemented notwithstanding any time limits in their domestic law.

155.   No peer input was provided during stage 1.

Recent developments

Bilateral modifications

156.   There are no recent developments as to new treaties or amendments to existing treaties being signed in relation to element D.3.

Peer input

157.   No peer input was provided.

Anticipated modifications

158.   The Bahamas reported it will seek to include Article 25(2), second sentence, of the OECD Model Tax Convention (OECD, 2017) or both alternatives in all of its future tax treaties.

Conclusion

	Areas for improvement	Recommendations
[D.3]	-	-

Reference

OECD (2017), *Model Tax Convention on Income and on Capital 2017 (Full Version)*, OECD Publishing, Paris, https://dx.doi.org/10.1787/g2g972ee-en.

Summary

	Areas for improvement	Recommendations
Part A: Preventing disputes		
[A.1]	-	-
[A.2]	-	-
Part B: Availability and access to MAP		
[B.1]	-	-
[B.2]	-	-
[B.3]	-	-
[B.4]	-	-
[B.5]	-	-
[B.6]	-	-
[B.7]	-	-
[B.8]	There is no published MAP guidance.	The Bahamas should, without further delay, introduce and publish guidance on access to and use of the MAP, and in particular include the contact information of its competent authority as well as the manner and form in which the taxpayer should submit its MAP request, including the documentation and information that should be included in such a request.
[B.9]	There is no MAP guidance publicly available. Furthermore, the MAP profile of the Bahamas contains only limited information.	The Bahamas should make its MAP guidance publicly available and easily accessible once it has been introduced. Furthermore, the Bahamas should provide further details in its MAP profile.
[B.10]	-	-
Part C: Resolution of MAP cases		
[C.1]	-	-
[C.2]	-	-
[C.3]	-	-
[C.4]	-	-
[C.5]	-	-
[C.6]	-	-
Part D: Implementation of MAP agreements		
[D.1]	-	-
[D.2]	-	-
[D.3]	-	-

Annex A

Tax treaty network of the Bahamas

Treaty partner	DTC in force?	If N, date of signing	Article 25(1) of the OECD Model Tax Convention ("MTC")		Article 9(2) of the OECD MTC	Anti-abuse	Article 25(2) of the OECD MTC		Article 25(3) of the OECD MTC		Arbitration
			Inclusion Art. 25(1) first sentence? / If yes, submission to either competent authority? (new Art. 25(1), first sentence) — B.1	Inclusion Art. 25(1) second sentence? (Note 1) / If no, please state reasons / iii if ii, specify period — B.1	Inclusion Art. 9(2) (Note 2) If no, will your CA provide access to MAP in TP cases? — B.3	Inclusion provision that MAP Article will not be available in cases where your jurisdiction is of the assessment that there is an abuse of the DTC or of the domestic tax law? / If no, will your CA accept a taxpayer's request for MAP in relation to such cases? — B.4	Inclusion Art. 25(2) first sentence? (Note 3) — C.1	Inclusion Art. 25(2) second sentence? (Note 4) / If no, alternative provision in Art. 7 & 9 OECD MTC? (Note 4) — D.3	Inclusion Art. 25(3) first sentence? (Note 5) — A.1	Inclusion Art. 25(3) second sentence? (Note 6) — B.7	Inclusion arbitration provision? — C.6
	Y = yes / N = signed pending ratification		E = yes, either CAs / O = yes, only one CA / N = No	Y = yes / i = no, no such provision / ii = no, different period / iii = no, starting point for computing the 3 year period is different / iv = no, other reasons	Y = yes / i = no, but access will be given to TP cases / ii = no and access will not be given to TP cases	Y = yes / i = no and such cases will be accepted for MAP / ii = no but such cases will not be accepted for MAP	Y = yes / N = no	Y = yes / i = no, but have Art. 7 equivalent / ii = no, but have Art. 9 equivalent / iii = no, but have both Art. 7 & 9 equivalent / N = no and no equivalent of Art. 7 and 9	Y = yes / N = no	Y = yes / N = no	Y = yes / N = no
	Column 2		Column 3	Column 4	Column 5	Column 6	Column 7	Column 8	Column 9	Column 10	Column 11
Column 1											
Japan	Y	N/A	O	Y (N/A)	N/A	i	Y	Y	Y	N	N

Annex B

MAP Statistics Reporting for pre-2017 cases (1 January 2017 to 31 December 2020)

2017 MAP Statistics

Category of cases	No. of pre-2017 cases in MAP inventory on 1 January 2017	Denied MAP access	Objection is not justified	Withdrawn by taxpayer	Unilateral relief granted	Resolved via domestic remedy	Agreement fully eliminating double taxation/fully resolving taxation not in accordance with tax treaty	Agreement partially eliminating double taxation/partially resolving taxation not in accordance with tax treaty	Agreement that there is no taxation not in accordance with tax treaty	No agreement, including agreement to disagree	Any other outcome	No. of pre-2017 cases remaining in on MAP inventory on 31 December 2017	Average time taken (in months) for closing pre-2017 cases during the reporting period
	Column 2	Column 3	Column 4	Column 5	Column 6	Column 7	Column 8	Column 9	Column 10	Column 11	Column 12	Column 13	Column 14
Attribution/ Allocation	0	0	0	0	0	0	0	0	0	0	0	0	N/A
Others	0	0	0	0	0	0	0	0	0	0	0	0	N/A
Total	0	0	0	0	0	0	0	0	0	0	0	0	N/A

2018 MAP Statistics

Category of cases	No. of pre-2017 cases in MAP inventory on 1 January 2018	Denied MAP access	Objection is not justified	Withdrawn by taxpayer	Unilateral relief granted	Resolved via domestic remedy	Agreement fully eliminating double taxation/fully resolving taxation not in accordance with tax treaty	Agreement partially eliminating double taxation/partially resolving taxation not in accordance with tax treaty	Agreement that there is no taxation not in accordance with tax treaty	No agreement, including agreement to disagree	Any other outcome	No. of pre-2017 cases remaining in on MAP inventory on 31 December 2018	Average time taken (in months) for closing pre-2017 cases during the reporting period
	Column 2	Column 3	Column 4	Column 5	Column 6	Column 7	Column 8	Column 9	Column 10	Column 11	Column 12	Column 13	Column 14
Attribution/ Allocation	0	0	0	0	0	0	0	0	0	0	0	0	N/A
Others	0	0	0	0	0	0	0	0	0	0	0	0	N/A
Total	0	0	0	0	0	0	0	0	0	0	0	0	N/A

2019 MAP Statistics

Category of cases	No. of pre-2017 cases in MAP inventory on 1 January 2019	Number of pre-2017 cases closed during the reporting period by outcome										No. of pre-2017 cases remaining in on MAP inventory on 31 December 2019	Average time taken (in months) for closing pre-2017 cases during the reporting period
		Denied MAP access	Objection is not justified	Withdrawn by taxpayer	Unilateral relief granted	Resolved via domestic remedy	Agreement fully eliminating double taxation/ fully resolving taxation not in accordance with tax treaty	Agreement partially eliminating double taxation/partially resolving taxation not in accordance with tax treaty	Agreement that there is no taxation not in accordance with tax treaty	No agreement, including agreement to disagree	Any other outcome		
Column 1	Column 2	Column 3	Column 4	Column 5	Column 6	Column 7	Column 8	Column 9	Column 10	Column 11	Column 12	Column 13	Column 14
Attribution/ Allocation	0	0	0	0	0	0	0	0	0	0	0	0	N/A
Others	0	0	0	0	0	0	0	0	0	0	0	0	N/A
Total	0	0	0	0	0	0	0	0	0	0	0	0	N/A

2020 MAP Statistics

Category of cases	No. of pre-2017 cases in MAP inventory on 1 January 2020	Number of pre-2017 cases closed during the reporting period by outcome										No. of pre-2017 cases remaining in on MAP inventory on 31 December 2020	Average time taken (in months) for closing pre-2017 cases during the reporting period
		Denied MAP access	Objection is not justified	Withdrawn by taxpayer	Unilateral relief granted	Resolved via domestic remedy	Agreement fully eliminating double taxation/ fully resolving taxation not in accordance with tax treaty	Agreement partially eliminating double taxation/partially resolving taxation not in accordance with tax treaty	Agreement that there is no taxation not in accordance with tax treaty	No agreement, including agreement to disagree	Any other outcome		
Column 1	Column 2	Column 3	Column 4	Column 5	Column 6	Column 7	Column 8	Column 9	Column 10	Column 11	Column 12	Column 13	Column 14
Attribution/ Allocation	0	0	0	0	0	0	0	0	0	0	0	0	N/A
Others	0	0	0	0	0	0	0	0	0	0	0	0	N/A
Total	0	0	0	0	0	0	0	0	0	0	0	0	N/A

Annex C

MAP Statistics Reporting for post-2016 cases
(1 January 2017 to 31 December 2020)

2017 MAP Statistics

Category of cases	No. of post-2016 cases in MAP inventory on 1 January 2017	No. of post-2016 cases started during the reporting period	Number of post-2016 cases closed during the reporting period by outcome										No. of post-2016 cases remaining in on MAP inventory on 31 December 2017	Average time taken (in months) for closing post-2016 cases during the reporting period
			Denied MAP access	Objection is not justified	Withdrawn by taxpayer	Unilateral relief granted	Resolved via domestic remedy	Agreement fully eliminating double taxation/ fully resolving taxation not in accordance with tax treaty	Agreement partially eliminating double taxation/partially resolving taxation not in accordance with tax treaty	Agreement that there is no taxation not in accordance with tax treaty	No agreement, including agreement to disagree	Any other outcome		
Column 1	Column 2	Column 3	Column 4	Column 5	Column 6	Column 7	Column 8	Column 9	Column 10	Column 11	Column 12	Column 13	Column 14	Column 15
Attribution/ Allocation	0	0	0	0	0	0	0	0	0	0	0	0	0	N/A
Others	0	0	0	0	0	0	0	0	0	0	0	0	0	N/A
Total	0	0	0	0	0	0	0	0	0	0	0	0	0	N/A

2018 MAP Statistics

Category of cases	No. of post-2016 cases in MAP inventory on 1 January 2018	No. of post-2016 cases started during the reporting period	Number of post-2016 cases closed during the reporting period by outcome										No. of post-2016 cases remaining in on MAP inventory on 31 December 2018	Average time taken (in months) for closing post-2016 cases during the reporting period
			Denied MAP access	Objection is not justified	Withdrawn by taxpayer	Unilateral relief granted	Resolved via domestic remedy	Agreement fully eliminating double taxation/ fully resolving taxation not in accordance with tax treaty	Agreement partially eliminating double taxation/partially resolving taxation not in accordance with tax treaty	Agreement that there is no taxation not in accordance with tax treaty	No agreement, including agreement to disagree	Any other outcome		
Column 1	Column 2	Column 3	Column 4	Column 5	Column 6	Column 7	Column 8	Column 9	Column 10	Column 11	Column 12	Column 13	Column 14	Column 15
Attribution/ Allocation	0	0	0	0	0	0	0	0	0	0	0	0	0	N/A
Others	0	0	0	0	0	0	0	0	0	0	0	0	0	N/A
Total	0	0	0	0	0	0	0	0	0	0	0	0	0	N/A

2019 MAP Statistics

Category of cases	No. of post-2016 cases in MAP inventory on 1 January 2019	No. of post-2016 cases started during the reporting period	Number of post-2016 cases closed during the reporting period by outcome											No. of post-2016 cases remaining in on MAP inventory on 31 December 2019	Average time taken (in months) for closing post-2016 cases during the reporting period
			Denied MAP access	Objection is not justified	Withdrawn by taxpayer	Unilateral relief granted	Resolved via domestic remedy	Agreement fully eliminating double taxation/ fully resolving taxation not in accordance with tax treaty	Agreement partially eliminating double taxation/partially resolving taxation not in accordance with tax treaty	Agreement that there is no taxation not in accordance with tax treaty	No agreement, including agreement to disagree	Any other outcome		
Column 1	Column 2	Column 3	Column 4	Column 5	Column 6	Column 7	Column 8	Column 9	Column 10	Column 11	Column 12	Column 13	Column 14	Column 15
Attribution/ Allocation	0	0	0	0	0	0	0	0	0	0	0	0	0	N/A
Others	0	0	0	0	0	0	0	0	0	0	0	0	0	N/A
Total	0	0	0	0	0	0	0	0	0	0	0	0	0	N/A

2020 MAP Statistics

Category of cases	No. of post-2016 cases in MAP inventory on 1 January 2020	No. of post-2016 cases started during the reporting period	Number of post-2016 cases closed during the reporting period by outcome											No. of post-2016 cases remaining in on MAP inventory on 31 December 2020	Average time taken (in months) for closing post-2016 cases during the reporting period
			Denied MAP access	Objection is not justified	Withdrawn by taxpayer	Unilateral relief granted	Resolved via domestic remedy	Agreement fully eliminating double taxation/ fully resolving taxation not in accordance with tax treaty	Agreement partially eliminating double taxation/partially resolving taxation not in accordance with tax treaty	Agreement that there is no taxation not in accordance with tax treaty	No agreement, including agreement to disagree	Any other outcome		
Column 1	Column 2	Column 3	Column 4	Column 5	Column 6	Column 7	Column 8	Column 9	Column 10	Column 11	Column 12	Column 13	Column 14	Column 15
Attribution/ Allocation	0	0	0	0	0	0	0	0	0	0	0	0	0	N/A
Others	0	0	0	0	0	0	0	0	0	0	0	0	0	N/A
Total	0	0	0	0	0	0	0	0	0	0	0	0	0	N/A

Glossary

Action 14 Minimum Standard	The minimum standard as agreed upon in the final report on Action 14: Making Dispute Resolution Mechanisms More Effective
MAP Statistics Reporting Framework	Rules for reporting of MAP statistics as agreed by the FTA MAP Forum
OECD Model Tax Convention	OECD Model Tax Convention on Income and on Capital as it read on 21 November 2017
OECD Transfer Pricing Guidelines	OECD Transfer Pricing Guidelines for Multinational Enterprises and Tax Administrations
Pre-2017 cases	MAP cases in a competent authority's inventory that are pending resolution on 31 December 2016
Post-2016 cases	MAP cases that are received by a competent authority from the taxpayer on or after 1 January 2017
Statistics Reporting Period	Period for reporting MAP statistics that started on 1 January 2017 and ended on 31 December 2020
Terms of Reference	Terms of reference to monitor and review the implementing of the BEPS Action 14 Minimum Standard to make dispute resolution mechanisms more effective

www.ingramcontent.com/pod-product-compliance
Lightning Source LLC
Chambersburg PA
CBHW062030210326
41519CB00060B/7373